# Table of Contents

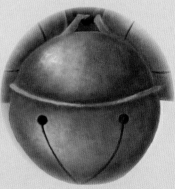

# Sources

**The Creative Touch**
Phone: 508-485-9306
Web: www.thecreativetouch.com

**J.B. Wood, Inc.**
Phone: 800-859-4668
Web: www.jbwood.com

**Painter's Paradise**
Phone: 302-798-3897
Web: www.paintersparadise.com

**Viking Woodcrafts, Inc.**
Phone: 800-328-0116
Web: www.vikingwoodcrafts.com

**Wood Concepts**
Phone: 888-327-8996
Web: www.woodconceptsstudio.com

# Brushes

**Loew-Cornell®, Series:**
4 duster
32 fan
244 angular bristle
270 mop
272 dome round
410 deerfoot
1178 large area brush
2014 round scumbler
7000 round
7050 liner
7120 rake
7300 flat shader
7350 liner
7400 angle shader
7500 filbert
7520 filbert rake
7550 flat wash
7600 oval wash
1/8" lettering brush

## Published and Distributed by

Viking Woodcrafts, Inc.
1317 8th St. SE
Waseca, MN 56093
1-800-328-0116
www.vikingwoodcrafts.com

## Printed by

J-C Press, Owatonna, MN

## Layout & Design

As Is Design, Inc., Waseca, MN

## Photography

Jon Lucca., Waseca, MN

# General Instructions and Painting Terms

### Dry Brush

A technique used to highlight or shade an area. Load just the tips of a scumbler brush with paint, then pounce lightly on the disposable palette. Remove the excess paint by softly stroking the brush over dry paper toweling. Apply paint to surface with light pressure, using a circular motion.

### Extender/Drying Retarder

Extender and retarder are mediums that allow you to work and blend acrylic paints for longer periods of time. The retarder can be used to moisten the brush for better paint blending on a dry surface, or it can be applied to the surface, over the section of the design to be painted wet-to-wet. Spread the medium over the surface with a large flat brush. "Stretch" it out by pulling it over the surface in many directions, leaving a thin layer. The surface should look damp, not wet. Paint the area according to the instructions. Should the area become tacky before you are finished, dry the piece with a hair dryer. When completely dry and cool, reapply the extender/retarder and complete the technique. It is recommended to seal off finished wood designs with a clear glaze or matte spray sealer prior to varnishing.

### Finishing

All projects must be varnished before they are complete. Study the project to determine that all shadows and highlighting are balanced. Check to see that all the details are sharp and lines are straight. Be sure to erase any transfer lines that may be showing, using a soft kneaded eraser. Wipe the surface with a clean tack cloth. Finish the piece with a water-based brush-on or wipe-on varnish. A matte finish will provide low luster, satin will show a slight glow, and gloss varnish will have a bright shine. Apply two or more coats with a good-quality brush. Rub with a wood finishing pad, such as a Super Film pad, wipe with a tack cloth, and apply a last coat of varnish. For best results using a wipe-on varnish, apply 10-15 coats. A good applicator is an automotive polishing pad. Keep the applicator zipped up in a plastic bag between applications to keep the surface moist and ready.

### Scumbling

Used to create form, texture, and accents. Load the scumbler brush with a moderate amount of paint, then pounce lightly on the disposable palette to evenly distribute the paint. Apply to the painting surface in a circular motion for form and accents or in a back and forth motion to create texture on backgrounds.

### Sideload Float

Choose a flat brush with a good chisel edge. First dip the brush into clean water. Blot on paper toweling to remove the excess water, just until the "sheen" goes away. Dip the corner of the brush into the paint and blend, back and forth in one spot, on the palette, until the water and paint merge in the middle. The amount of water in the brush is vital. If the paint drags during the blending, you need more water. If the water beads up, there is too much water in the brush. Practice this until you get the feel of how much water to use.

### Slip-slap

Slip-slap technique is used to create an interesting background. It is painted with a filbert to keep the edges soft. Load the brush with the color indicated in the instructions, then pull the brush in short strokes to create "Xs." For applying multiple colors, work with a dirty brush, adding each color wet-to-wet. For a soft, transparent background, apply a coat of clear glazing medium to the surface first, and add some clear glazing medium to the brush.

### Spatter (fly-specking)

Used to apply snow, an aged look, or an accent to painted designs. Moisten a fan brush with water, and thin paint to an ink consistency. Fully load the fan brush with the thinned paint. Hold the brush about 6" above the surface to be spattered. Hold the brush firmly, in a horizontal position. Hit the ferrule sharply with the handle of a palette knife to spatter small paint spots over the painting. Be sure to practice before applying to the painted piece.

### Stippling

Used for creating trees, bushes, and some flowers. A deerfoot or angular bristle brush are recommended. Load the brush with paint, then pounce lightly on the disposable palette. Stipple (pounce) in an up-and-down motion with a light touch. When stippling multiple colors, start with the middle value, then stipple in the dark and light while the first color is wet. Work all the colors in one section at a time. This helps to create many shades of color.

### Wet-to-wet

Working multiple colors together while they are wet to blend the colors in a more subtle way. Stippling techniques are one example of this. Painting wet-to-wet is often used to add shadows, highlights, or tints over the background color before it dries.

# American Red Start

## Pallette
**DecoArt Americana**
Arbor Green
Avocado Dip
Cadmium Orange
Cadmium Yellow
Camel
Grey Sky
Marigold
Milk Chocolate
Neutral Grey
Plantation Pine
Soft Black
Titanium White
Violet Haze
Warm White

## Mediums
DecoArt Brush 'N Blend Extender
DecoArt Faux Glazing Medium

## Loew-Cornell Brushes
#1, #4 round
#0, #6/0, #18/0 liner
#2, #4, #6, #8, filbert
1/8'', 1/4'', 1/2'' angle shader
3/4'' oval wash
#2 scumbler
1/4'' rake
#2 duster
1'' basecoat

## Surface
Item #530, Decorative Panel,
J.B. Wood, Inc.

## Supplies
Fine-grit sandpaper
Tack cloth
Tracing paper
Transfer paper
Clear glaze or matte
  spray sealer

# Preparation

Sand and seal the panel. Using the 1" basecoat brush, paint the insert with Camel. When dry, slip-slap the background on both sides with a 3/4" oval wash: glaze, Camel, Cadmium Orange, and Arbor Green. Paint the trim Soft Black. When dry, use the #2 duster to lightly dry brush Violet Haze over the trim.

Trace the pattern onto tracing paper and transfer onto the panel.

# Branches

Paint the branches with a #4 round loaded with Neutral Grey + Violet Haze 3:1. Shade the large branches, along the bottom and where one comes out from behind another, with an #8 filbert moistened with Extender and sideloaded into the base mix + Soft Black 1:1. Use a #1 round to shadow the small branches and twigs. Highlight in the same manner with Grey Sky.

# Leaves

Paint the green leaves with Arbor Green. Apply a thin layer of Extender over each leaf. Sideload a 1/2" angle shader, which has been moistened with Extender, with Plantation Pine. Shade at the base and in the center at the vein line. While wet, add highlights with Avocado Dip.

Paint the yellow leaves Marigold. Shade with Cadmium Orange + Milk Chocolate 2:1; highlight with Cadmium Yellow. The stems are painted with a #0 liner loaded with Plantation Pine.

# Birds

The birds are fluffed in with a #6 filbert that has been moistened in Extender. The head and lower body are Neutral Grey + Violet Haze 3:1. The breast is Grey Sky. The shoulder patch near the wing, the stripes on the wing, and tail are Marigold + a touch of Cadmium Orange. The remainder of the wing and tail are Neutral Grey and Soft Black 1:1.

The second layer is painted wet-to-wet to create the down and feathers. Apply a thin coat of Extender to the bird. Moisten a #4 filbert with Extender and load the brush, using the same colors. Fluff in the colors with soft, short, shape-forming strokes. Let dry completely.

The third layer is painted with a 1/4" rake brush. Moisten the brush with water. Load the brush with Grey Sky and apply short, feathery strokes to the head and upper and lower chest; pick up Warm White and add strokes to the breast. Use Soft Black on the dark areas of the wing and tail, Marigold on the stripes. Add Marigold + Warm White to the shoulder patch.

# Details

Add lines with a #6/0 liner loaded with thinned paint: Marigold + a touch of Cadmium Orange on all parts of the wing and tail, Warm White on the shoulder patch.

# Eyes

Paint the eyes Soft Black. Highlight the left side with a 1/8" angle shader sideloaded with Violet Haze. Add a shine dot with Warm White in the upper highlight area. Add dots with an #18/0 liner loaded with thinned Warm White along the bottom outside the eye, the top with Grey Sky + Warm White 1:1. Pull a few lines from the back of the eye onto the head with Violet Haze + Soft Black 3:1.

## Beak

Neutral Grey. Shade with a 1/8" angle brush sideloaded with Soft Black. Add some dry brush highlights with a #2 scumbler sparsely loaded with Grey Sky. Add a few tiny lines onto the face and neck with Soft Black + Neutral Grey 1:1.

## Feet

Paint the feet with a #1 round double-loaded with Neutral Grey and Soft Black. Pull a few highlights here and there with Grey Sky.

## Berries

Paint the berries with a #2 filbert loaded with Plantation Pine + Avocado Dip 1:1. Shade with a 1/4" angle shader, moistened in Extender and sideloaded with Plantation Pine. Highlight with Avocado dip. When dry, tint some berries with Cadmium Orange. Add shine dots with Titanium White. Add stems with Neutral Grey + Violet Haze 3:1.

## Finishing

Seal off the finished design with a clear glaze or matte spray sealer prior to varnishing. For more information, see Painting Terms.

Autumn Serenity

## Palette

**DecoArt**

**Americana**

Black Green
Bleached Sand
Bright Orange
Burnt Umber
Cadmium Orange
Cadmium Yellow
Citron
French Vanilla
Hauser Light Green
Milk Chocolate
Napa Red
Neutral Grey
Plantation Pine
Raw Sienna
Russet
Tangerine
Titanium White

## Mediums

Weathered Wood
DecoArt Brush 'N
 Blend Extender
J.W. Etc. UnderCover
 white

## Supplies

Fine-grit sandpaper
Tracing paper
Transfer paper
Vinegar
Soft cloth

## Surface

Item #35-9719, 12" square tin tile with leaf border and item #20-10597, 1 1/2" frame, available from Viking Woodcrafts, Inc.

## Loew-Cornell Brushes

#1, #3 round
#0 liner
#8, #6, #10 flat
#2, #4, #12 filbert
#4 fan
1/2" angular bristle
#2, #8 scumbler
1/8" deerfoot
2" basecoat

# Autumn Serenity

## Preparation

Sand and seal the frame. Paint with Russet. Wash the tin tile with vinegar and water 5:1. Let dry completely. Apply a good, even coat of UnderCover. Let dry completely. Paint the tile with two coats of French Vanilla.

Trace the pattern onto tracing paper. Transfer the horizon line onto the tile.

## Background Foliage

Apply a thin coat of Extender to the area. Moisten the #12 filbert with Extender, and load the brush with Plantation Pine. Slip-slap over the foliage area. Pick up Black Green and slip-slap on the left and slightly into the right side. While wet, stipple over the area with a 1/2" angular bristle: Plantation Pine, Black Green toward bottom and left, Hauser Light Green toward top and right, and Cadmium Orange in middle areas mostly on the right. Add more Cadmium Orange to brighten the area here and there. Keep the application light, allowing the background to show through.

## Grasses

Moisten a #4 fan with Extender. Load the brush with French Vanilla and tap into the ground area. Pick up Hauser Light Green and tap over the first color; add more of this color into the middle and right. Add some Cadmium Orange toward the bottom and here and there on the left. Look to the photo for placement. Let it all dry thoroughly.

## Chair

Apply the pattern outlines of the chair. Paint the chair with Russet. When dry, apply a good coat of Weathered Wood according to directions on the bottle. Carefully paint over the Weathered Wood with Bleached Sand. Crackling should begin to show within a few minutes. Let it all dry completely. Transfer the remaining pattern lines.

Create the separations of the boards on the back and the chair's seat with a #0 liner loaded with thinned Neutral Grey. Keep these lines soft. Wash in shadows under the arm of the chair, the cut ends of the boards, and the sides of the arms with a #10 flat loaded with Neutral Grey + water 1:1. Highlight the chair with a #10 flat sideloaded with Titanium White on the top right of each slat on the back, the front part of the arms, the right side of all vertical boards, and on the front of the chair. Squiggle a little Titanium White on the shaded part of the chair back.

## Birdhouse

Paint the walls of the birdhouse Milk Chocolate and the roof Milk Chocolate + Raw Sienna 1:1. Paint the vertical lines and the hole with thinned Black Green. Shade under the roof, right side walls, and the top of the roof with an #8 flat sideloaded with Black Green. Highlight the walls and the roof with Raw Sienna + French Vanilla 1:1. Add highlight strokes on the cut edge of the roof and dowel top with a #0 liner loaded with French Vanilla.

## Basket

Paint the basket Milk Chocolate. Shade to separate the reed with a #6 flat sideloaded with Black Green. Shade along the bottom and right side of the basket with an #8 flat sideloaded with Black Green. Highlight the left sides of the reed with Raw Sienna + French Vanilla 1:1.

Paint the handle and the small reed that goes around the basket with a #0 liner loaded with Milk Chocolate. Overstroke a highlight with Milk Chocolate + French Vanilla 1:1. Add some brighter strokes with French Vanilla here and there.

## Flowers

The greenery for the flowers in the basket and on the ground is stippled with a 1/8" deerfoot loaded with Plantation Pine. Pull stems with a #0 liner loaded with thinned Plantation Pine. Let dry. Paint leaves with a #2 filbert double-loaded with Plantation Pine and Citron.

The yellow flowers in the basket are painted with a #2 filbert double-loaded with Cadmium Yellow and French Vanilla; the red flowers are painted with the brush double-loaded with Russet and Bleached Sand. The rose flowers are painted with a #1 round fully loaded with Napa Red and tipped into Titanium White. The orange flowers

are tapped in with Cadmium Orange and Titanium White on the tip. The Mums are stippled in with a 1/8" deerfoot loaded with Tangerine on the short end and Cadmium Yellow on the long end. Add some brighter highlights on the top of the flower with French Vanilla.

## Pumpkin

Basecoat the pumpkin with Bright Orange + a touch of Citron. Paint in the rib lines with a #0 liner loaded with Russet. Scumble over the pumpkin lightly with Tangerine. Moisten the pumpkin with Extender. Shade the right side with a #10 flat sideloaded with Cadmium Orange, and deepen the shading with Cadmium Orange + Russet 2:1. Highlight the left side with Tangerine + Cadmium Yellow 1:1.

## Stem

Paint the pumpkin stem with Raw Sienna. Scumble over with a #2 scumbler sparsely loaded with French Vanilla. Shade with an #8 flat sideloaded with Black Green. Tint the top with Cadmium Orange.

## Tree Branches and Leaves

Paint the tree branches with a #3 round loaded with Burnt Umber. All the leaves are painted with a #2 filbert that has been moistened in Extender. Pull three small strokes for each leaf. Use a variety of colors chosen from the oranges and yellows.

## Leaf Border

Antique the leaf border with Russet + Extender 1:1. Brush the antiquing mixture over the leaf border; while wet, wipe off raised parts of the leaves with a soft cloth. Let dry completely. Scumble over the tops of the leaves with an #8 scumbler sparsely loaded with Bleached Sand.

## Finishing

Seal off the finished design with a clear glaze or matte spray sealer prior to varnishing. For more information, see Painting Terms.

# Butterflies and Lace

## Palette
**DecoArt Americana**
Boysenberry
Burgundy Wine
Dove Grey
Lamp Black
Neutral Grey
Warm White

## Mediums
DecoArt Brush 'N Blend Extender
DecoArt Faux Glazing Medium
Matte spray sealer

## Loew-Cornell Brushes
#3 round
#0, #6/0 liner
#12 flat
#6, #10 filbert
1" oval wash
#4, #6 scumbler

## Supplies
Tracing paper
Transfer paper

## Surface
Item #208105993, Cluny
Lace tin plate, available from
Painter's Paradise and from
Viking Woodcrafts, Inc., Item
#145-0027.

## Preparation
Seal the plate with a light coat of matte spray sealer.

## Background Hazing
Slip-slap the background with a 1" oval wash: Faux Glazing Medium, Warm White, Dove Grey, and Boysenberry. Let dry completely. Trace the pattern onto tracing paper, and transfer the outlines onto the plate.

## Pussy Willows
Paint the pussy willows with a #6 filbert moistened with Extender and loaded with Dove Grey. Pull the stems with a #6/0 liner loaded with thinned Neutral Grey.

## Flowers
Basecoat the flowers with Warm White + Dove Grey 2:1. When dry, apply a thin coat of Extender over each flower. Shade each flower petal with a #10 filbert sideloaded with Dove Grey. Add the first highlight with a #10 filbert sideloaded with Warm White.

Deepen the shadows with Dove Grey + Boysenberry 2:1. Pull some lines out from the center onto each petal with a #0 liner loaded with thinned Dove Grey + Boysenberry 2:1. Reinforce the highlights with Warm White. Place the stamen in the center of the flower with a #3 round moistened in Extender and loaded with Warm White.

The stems are painted with a #3 round double-loaded with Dove Grey and Neutral Grey.

Add some illusion flowers in the background with a #10 filbert loaded with Warm White + Faux Glazing Medium 2:1.

## Butterfly
Paint the butterfly wings with Boysenberry + Warm White 2:1. Shade next to the body and the top of the wing with a #12 flat sideloaded with Boysenberry. Deepen the shading with Burgundy Wine.

The antennae, body, and all the vein lines are painted with a #0 liner; but use a #6/0 liner loaded with Lamp Black for small lines.

Highlights on the wings are scumbled with a #6 scumbler sparsely loaded with Warm White + a touch of Boysenberry. The highlights on the body are scumbled with a #4 scumbler sparsely loaded with Dove Grey.

Add white dots on the body and wings with Warm White.

## Finishing
For more on finishing, see Painting Terms.

## Palette

**DecoArt Americana**

Antique Teal
Black Green
Black Plum
Brilliant Red
Burnt Sienna
Cadmium Yellow
Canyon Orange
Citron
Evergreen
Forest Green
Georgia Clay
Hauser Dark Green
Hauser Light Green
Lamp Black
Lemon Yellow
Light Avocado
Napa Red
Raw Sienna
Rookwood
Tangerine
Teal
Titanium White

## Mediums

DecoArt Brush 'N Blend Extender
DecoArt Faux Glazing Medium

## Supplies

Fine-grit sandpaper
Tracing paper
Transfer paper
Paper towels

## Loew-Cornell Brushes

#0 liner
#10, #12, 1" flat
#4, #12 filbert
1/4" angle shader
1" oval wash
1/4" rake
Large dome round
2" basecoat

## Surface

Witch Box, 16" X 7" X 3 1/2",
available from Wood Concepts.

# Citrus Medley

## Preparation

Sand and seal the wood. The lid is painted with Antique Teal. Only one coat is needed. Slip-slap the background on the lid with a 1" oval wash using Antique Teal, Teal, and Faux Glazing Medium medium. Let dry completely.

The remainder of the box is painted Raw Sienna. When dry, dampen with water and apply a glaze of Burnt Sienna + Faux Glazing Medium 1:1. While wet, blot with a damp paper towel to create a mottled look. Let dry. Dampen and apply the Burnt Sienna glaze mix here and there, and blot with a damp paper towel. Let dry. Dampen again with water and apply a glaze of Black Plum + Faux Glazing Medium 1:2. Blot with paper towel. Let dry. Apply darker spots with a 1" flat sideloaded with Burnt Sienna + a touch of Lamp Black. Blot with paper towel.

Trace the pattern onto tracing paper. Transfer onto the lid of the box.

Basecoat all the citrus fruit with Titanium White. Wash over the limes with Hauser Light Green and the orange with Lemon Yellow. The paint is mixed with water 60/40 to create a transparent wash.

## General Information

All shadows and highlights are painted with wet-to-wet blending, using Extender. Start with a light application of Extender on the surface, and moisten the brush with Extender before picking up the paint.

## Leaves

Paint the leaves with Light Avocado. Shade with a #12 flat sideloaded with Evergreen + Black Green 1:1. Highlight the leaves with a 1/4" rake brush loaded with Citron. Moisten the brush with Extender, and thin the paint with Extender. Pull the rake across the leaf on the diagonal starting at the tip and moving toward the stem end. Continue to add layers until you are satisfied with the brightness. Let dry completely.

Reapply Extender and reinforce the shadows with Black Green.

## Fruit

The first layer of fruit is stippled with a dome round, over a surface that has been moistened with Extender.

The limes are stippled all over with Citron; pick up Forest Green and stipple the dark areas. Add Titanium White to the light areas.

The lemons are stippled in the same manner using Lemon Yellow over it all. Also use Cadmium Yellow in the dark areas and Titanium White in the light areas.

The orange is stippled all over with Tangerine. Add Canyon Orange + Georgia Clay 1:1 in the dark areas and Titanium White in the light areas.

## Shadows

Apply Extender to each fruit. Paint the shadows with a #12 filbert all along the bottom and sides of each fruit and lightly across the top. The orange has shading around the navel with a 1/4" angle shader. Pull out some strokes on the chisel edge of the brush. Use Hauser Dark Green on the limes, Burnt Sienna on the lemons, and Georgia Clay + Rookwood 3:1 on the orange. Let dry completely.

Apply Extender and deepen the shadows along the bottom and lower sides only. The limes are deepened with Black Green, the lemons with Burnt Sienna, and the orange with Rookwood + Georgia Clay 2:1.

## Tints

Add a tint of color to the fruit in the medium value on the upper right and the middle left. Tint the limes Lemon Yellow and the lemons and orange with Citron.

## Highlights

Brighten the fruit with a bull's eye highlight using a #12 filbert sideloaded with Titanium White.

The navel on the orange is outlined with a #0 liner loaded with thinned Rookwood + a touch of Citron. Tap some Citron into the center of the navel. Shade the navel along the bottom with Rookwood.

Add the deepest shadows on the fruit where one fruit comes out from behind another: limes with Black Green, lemons Burnt Sienna + a touch of Rookwood, and the orange with Rookwood.

## Berries

Paint the berries with Napa Red. Apply Extender and shade with a #10 flat sideloaded with Black Plum, all around the berry. Deepen the shadows with Black Plum along the stem end. Add a bull's eye highlight with a #4 filbert sideloaded with Brilliant Red. Reinforce the shadows along the stem end with Black Plum + Black Green 2:1. Reinforce the highlights with Brilliant Red + Tangerine 2:1. Stems are painted with a #0 liner double-loaded with thinned Burnt Sienna and Raw Sienna.

## Finishing

Seal off the finished design with a clear glaze or matte spray sealer prior to varnishing. Spatter with Georgia Clay + Rookwood 3:1. For more information, see Painting Terms.

## Palette

**DecoArt Americana**

Antique Gold
Bright Yellow
Burnt Umber Traditional
Cadmium Yellow
Evergreen
French Vanilla
Georgia Clay
Golden Straw
Graphite
Grey Sky
Hauser Medium Green
Leaf Green
Light Buttermilk
Light Parchment
Marigold
Olive Green
Payne's Grey
Salem Blue
Slate Grey
Tangerine
Terra Cotta
Warm White

## Mediums

DecoArt Brush 'N Blend Extender
DecoArt Faux Glazing Medium

## Supplies

Tracing paper
Transfer paper
J.W. Etc. Painter's Finishing Wax
Fine-grit sanding block
Paper towels

## Loew-Cornell Brushes

#4 round
#6/0, #0, #1, #2 liner
#8, #10, #12, #20, 1" flat
#4, #6, #10 filbert
3/8" angle shader
1/8" lettering
1/8", 1/4" deerfoot
#2, #6, #8 scumbler
#2 duster
2" basecoat

## Surface

17" X 14" plaque with 1/2" round bead trim, available from The Creative Touch.

## General Information

All shadows and highlights are painted over a surface that has been moistened with Extender, unless otherwise stated. Refer to Painting Terms at the front of this book for more information.

## Preparation

Sand and seal the piece. Paint the entire piece with Salem Blue. Apply Painter's Finishing Wax over the edges of the plaque and here and there on the frame portion of the plaque. Apply a generous coat of French Vanilla over this portion of the plaque. Let dry. Rub over the waxed areas with the sanding block to remove the layer of paint for a lightly distressed look. Paint the beaded trim Antique Gold. Brush over the top with an #8 scumbler sparsely loaded with French Vanilla, then Warm White.

Trace the pattern onto tracing paper and transfer the line to separate the wall and the table and the vertical lines on the wall.

## Background Wall

Paint double vertical lines with a #1 liner loaded with Payne's Grey. Paint a line of Warm White, immediately to the left of the first line.

Scumble Leaf Green with a #2 duster, lightly overall. Wash Payne's Grey + Water 1:1 overall with a 2" flat basecoat brush, and blot with a damp paper towel to create a slightly mottled look. Let dry.

## Table

Scumble over the table in a horizontal motion with a #2 duster sparsely loaded with Warm White. Shade along the left and bottom with a #20 flat sideloaded with Payne's Grey. Streak a few shadows in the center of the table. Add grain lines with a #0 liner loaded with thinned Payne's Grey.

## Flower Pots

The left pot on the top is basecoated using a 1" flat and French Vanilla. Add the drips with a #4 round loaded with a thinned mixture of Payne's Grey + Evergreen 1:1. See Step 1 on the worksheet. Let dry completely. Wash over the entire pot with a #20 flat loaded with Bright Yellow + water 1:1. While wet, streak some Antique Gold in vertical strokes down from the mouth of the pot, as in Step 2. Let dry. Apply a thin coat of Extender over the pot. Paint the shadows with a #20 flat (#10 flat for smaller areas), sideloaded with Antique Gold: See Step 3. Reinforce the shadows with Antique Gold + Evergreen 2:1 as in Step 4. Highlight the middle, spout, rims, and handles with Light Buttermilk, as in Step 5.

The pot on the left bottom is basecoated with Light Buttermilk. Scumble the first shadow along the top and left side with an #8 scumbler loaded with Grey Sky. Apply Extender and deepen the shadows with a #20 flat sideloaded with Slate Grey. Add highlights to the lower and right side with Warm White.

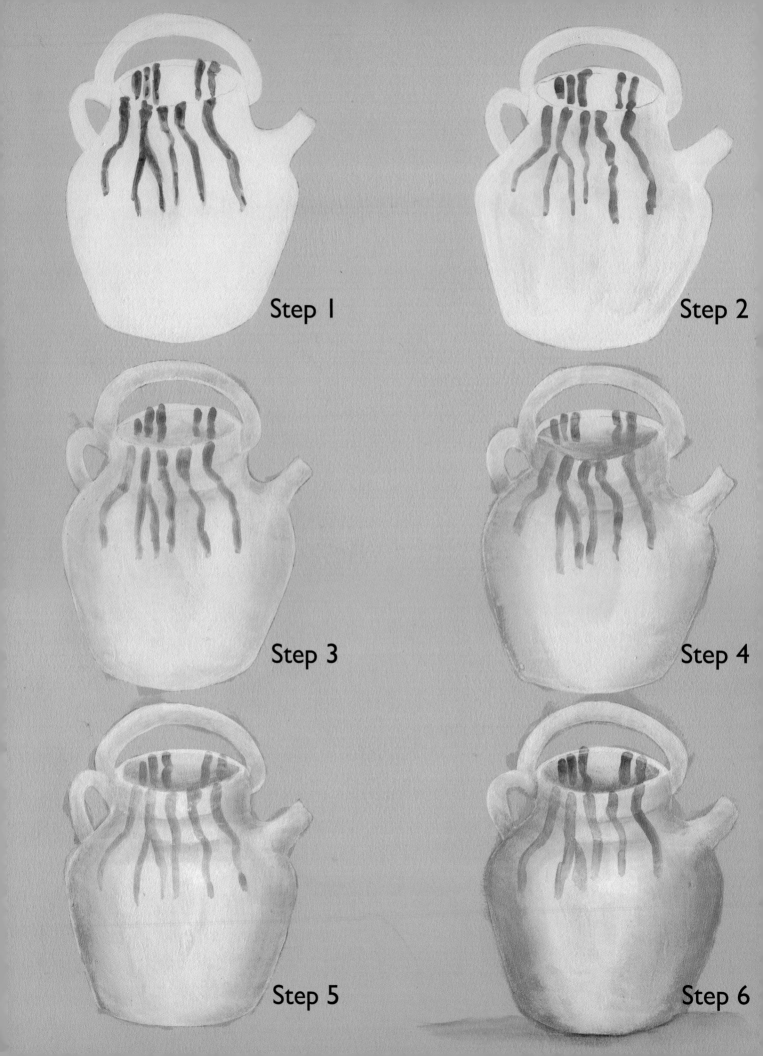

Step 1

Step 2

Step 3

Step 4

Step 5

Step 6

The middle pot is basecoated with Tangerine + Antique Gold 2:1 on the top, the bottom with Grey Sky. Scumble in the first shadows on the top with an #8 scrumbler loaded with Terra Cotta. Then pick up some Graphite on the dirty brush and scumble into the mouth of the pot. Wash over the top with Bright Yellow. Apply Extender. Deepen shadows with a #20 flat sideloaded with Terra Cotta. Add highlights with a #10 filbert sideloaded with Tangerine + Bright Yellow 1:1. Brighten the highlights with Light Buttermilk.

Basecoat the right pot with Light Parchment. Wash over it with Bright Yellow. Scumble in shadows with Hauser Medium Green. Apply Extender and paint shadows in Antique Gold. Add highlights with Light Buttermilk.

## Greenery
Stipple the greenery in the lower left pot with a 1/4'' deerfoot loaded with Evergreen. Add Hauser Medium Green and stipple over and above the first color. Add Olive Green toward the top. Pull stems and add delicate leaves with a #0 liner double-loaded with Evergreen and Olive Green.

## Marigolds
The marigold petals are painted with strokes pulled from the edge of the flower with a #6 filbert loaded with Antique Gold + Tangerine 1:1. Shade toward the centers with a #10 flat sideloaded with Georgia Clay. Highlight the tips with Cadmium Yellow. The centers are dots placed with a #0 liner loaded with Hauser Medium Green + Olive Green, loosely brush mixed.

## Leafy Sprig
Paint the stems and the leaf clusters with a #0 liner loaded with Evergreen. Stipple the tops with a 1/8'' deerfoot loaded with Evergreen. Progress to Olive Green, then Bright Yellow. Keep these light and airy.

## Zinnias
The zinnias are painted in three different tones. Light, medium, and dark. Instructions for all tones are the same. Basecoat the petals with a #6 filbert that has been moistened with Extender and fully loaded with the dark value. Paint the petals that are in the back two rows, then pick up the medium value and paint in the middle rows. Add the light value to the brush and paint the rows closest to the center.

## Light Flowers
Dark value: Golden Straw
Middle value: Cadmium Yellow
Light value: French Vanilla

## Medium Flowers
Dark value: Marigold + a touch of Golden Straw
Middle value: Golden Straw
Light value: French Vanilla

## Dark Flowers
Dark value: Marigold + Georgia Clay 1:1
Middle value: Marigold + Tangerine 2:1
Light value: Cadmium Yellow + French Vanilla 1:1

Add deeper shadows with a 3/8'' angle shader sideloaded with Marigold + Tangerine 2:1 on the light flowers, Marigold + Tangerine 1:1 for the medium flowers, and Marigold + Tangerine + Georgia Clay 1:1:1/2 for the dark flowers.

The centers of the zinnias are stippled in with a 1/8'' deerfoot. For light and medium flowers tap in Hauser Medium Green, then French Vanilla. For the dark flowers, tap in Georgia Clay, then French Vanilla.

## Sunflowers
The petals are painted with a #4 filbert loaded with Marigold. Shade with an #8 flat moistened in Extender and sideloaded with Marigold + Georgia Clay 3:1; highlight with French Vanilla.

The flower centers are basecoated with a #6 filbert loaded with Burnt Umber. While wet, pick up Payne's Grey on one side of the dirty brush and pit-pat shadows. Wipe the brush, and then pick up Extender and Georgia Clay. Pit-pat a highlight into the middle, and brighten the middle with French Vanilla.

## Golden Leaves
Basecoat the leaves with Antique Gold + Tangerine 2:1. Wash over with Cadmium Yellow. Shade the base and the center vein with a #12 flat sideloaded with Evergreen. Highlight with a #6 scrumbler sparsely loaded with French Vanilla. Add vein lines with a #6/0 liner loaded with thinned French Vanilla.

## Raffia
The raffia ball is painted with a #2 liner loaded with thinned French Vanilla for the darker strands. Next, pick up Light Buttermilk in the dirty brush and paint some medium strands over and between the dark. Add light strands with Warm White.

## Final Shadows
Apply a thin layer of Extender over the design area. With Payne's Grey, place shadows along the outside

edges of the pots, behind them, and in the deepest shadow areas on and in the mouths of the pots (see Step #6). Also shade under the pots, flowers, leaves, and the raffia with the same color.

## Lettering

Transfer the lettering to the frame. Paint each letter with a 1/8" lettering brush loaded with thinned Antique Gold. Brush in highlights with a #2 scumbler sparsely loaded with French Vanilla.

## Finishing

Seal off the finished design with a clear glaze or matte spray sealer prior to varnishing. For more information, see Painting Terms.

# Finishing Touches III

by Anne Hunter

Autumn Serenity
Pages 9-11
100% Scale

American Red Start
Pages 6-8
100% Scale

American Red Start
Pages 6-8
100% Scale
Pattern contines on next page

Pattern contines on next page

Welcome Lettering for
Spring and Winter Banners
50% Scale

American Red Start
Pages 6-8
100% Scale

Spring Welcome Banner
Pages 34-36
50% Scale

Skating on the Lake
Pages 30-33
100% Scale

Purple Finch
Pages 23-24
100% Scale

Butterflies and Lace
Pages 12-13
50% Scale

Winter Welcome Banner
Pages 37-39
50% Scale

Citrus Medley
Pages 14-15
60% Scale

Fruit-filled Lunch Box
Pages 21-22
100% Scale

Fleurs De Soleil
Pages 16-20
75% Scale

## Palette

**DecoArt Americana**

Antique Gold
Antique Green
Black Green
Black Plum
Blue Haze
Blue Mist
Bright Yellow
Burnt Sienna Traditional
Burnt Umber Traditional
Cadmium Orange
Cadmium Red
Cadmium Yellow
Lamp Black
Midnight Blue
Midnite Green
Napa Red
Olive Green
Oxblood
Payne's Grey
Raw Sienna
Royal Fuchsia
Warm White

## Mediums

DecoArt Brush 'N Blend Extender
Matte spray sealer

## Supplies

Tracing paper
Transfer paper

## Surface

Item #1115249, white tin lunch box, available from Painter's Paradise.

## Loew-Cornell Brushes

#1, #3 round
#10/0 liner
#12, #16, #20 flat
#6, #12 filbert
#4 duster

# Fruit-filled Lunch Box

## Preparation

The lunch box is pre-painted. Spray lightly with matte sealer. Trace the pattern onto tracing paper. Transfer the pattern outlines onto the piece. Apply a thin coat of Extender to the area behind the design and over the lid of the box. Shade all around the design and the lid with a #20 flat sideloaded with Black Green. Paint the top and bottom rims with Black Green.

## General Information

Shadows and highlights are applied over an area that has been moistened with Extender. Use a sideload technique with a brush that has been moistened with Extender before loading into paint.

## Leaves

Leaves are basecoated with Antique Green and shaded with Midnite Green with a #12 flat. Highlight with Antique Green + Olive Green 1:1. Vein lines are painted with a #10/0 liner loaded with Antique Green + Olive Green 1:1.

## Pear

Basecoat with Antique Gold. Shade with a #12 filbert sideloaded with Oxblood, then Oxblood + Burnt Umber 2:1. Highlight with Cadmium Yellow, Bright Yellow, and Warm White. The stem is painted with a #1 round double-loaded with Burnt Sienna and Midnite Green.

## Lemon

Paint the lemon with Cadmium Yellow. Shade with Burnt Sienna along the bottom with a #12 flat. Highlight the upper left of the lemon with Bright Yellow, then Bright Yellow + Warm White.

## Pomegranate

Basecoat the pomegranate with Royal Fuchsia. Shade with a #12 filbert sideloaded with Napa Red, then Black Plum. Look to the photo for placement. Highlight with a mix of Royal Fuchsia + Cadmium Orange 1:1. Let dry. Wash over the entire pomegranate with Cadmium Orange + water 1:1. Let dry. Add more highlights with Royal Fuchsia + Warm White 1:1. Dots inside the stem end are Black Plum, then Raw Sienna. Add a few additional dots of Cadmium Yellow to the right side.

## Grapes

Paint the grapes with a #6 filbert fully loaded with Midnight Blue. While wet, pick up Lamp Black on one side of the dirty brush and pit-pat to form the shadows. Add bull's eye highlights with Blue Haze, Blue Mist, and then Blue Mist + Warm White 1:1.

Stems and squiggles are painted with a #10/0 liner loaded with thinned Midnite Green and Olive Green.

## Final Shadows and Tints

Apply a light coat of Extender over the design, and while wet, add tints and final shadows.

Pear: Tint Cadmium Red on the upper portion of the light side.
Lemon: Tint with Olive Green next to the highlight area.

Deepen the shadows on the fruit in the darkest areas if needed:
Pear: Burnt Umber
Lemon: Burnt Sienna
Grapes: Lamp Black
Pomegranate: Payne's Grey

## Finishing

See Painting Terms.

Purple Finch

## Palette
**DecoArt Americana**
Cadmium Red
Charcoal
Dove Grey
Napa Red
Neutral Grey
Payne's Grey
Plantation Pine
Sapphire
Warm White

## Mediums
DecoArt Faux Glazing Medium
DecoArt Brush 'N Blend Extender

## Supplies
Tracing paper
Transfer paper

## Loew-Cornell Brushes
#1, #2, #4 round
1/4" angle shader
1/4" mop
#2 liner
#8 flat
#4, #6 filbert
3/4" oval wash

## Surface
Item #168-0014, Half Moon Vase, available from Viking Woodcrafts, Inc.

## Preparation
The vase is tinted Misty Grey and is paint-ready. With a 3/4" oval wash, slip-slap the background with Faux Glazing Medium, Dove Grey, Plantation Pine, Napa Red, and Sapphire. Trace the pattern onto tracing paper, and then transfer the outlines onto the vase.

## Branches
Basecoat the branches with a #4 round that is moistened in Extender and loaded with Dove Grey for the light areas. Pick up Neutral Grey and paint in the dark areas. Let dry. Apply a thin layer of Extender over the branches. Shade with a #6 filbert sideloaded with Charcoal; highlight with Warm White.

## Finch
The bird is painted in layers. The first layer is fluffed in using short, feathery strokes with a #6 filbert that has been moistened with Extender.

Paint Dove Grey on the head, front upper wing, breast, and the light part of the tail. Paint the rear wing tip, bottom of the wing, and the remainder of the tail Charcoal.

Add the stripes on the body with a #2 round, moistened in Extender and loaded with Neutral Grey. Pick up more Extender and Charcoal in the dirty brush, and deepen the stripes here and there.

The second layer is painted wet-to-wet with a #6 filbert to create the down and feathers. Apply a thin coat of Extender to the bird before painting. With Dove Grey, chop in feathers with the chisel edge of the brush on the head, breast, and body. Add Neutral Grey around the beak, next to the eye, and on the lower body next to the wing. Use long strokes for the light part of the tail. Add Charcoal to the wing and dark part of the tail. Let dry.

The third layer is painted with an #8 flat. Place "C" strokes on the head and breast with Cadmium Red. Deepen with strokes of Napa Red. Use a mop to soften. Brighten the breast with "C" strokes of Warm White, next to the Napa Red strokes for contrast. Place a few light feathers on the wing with chisel strokes of Warm White.

The feet and beak are painted with a #1 round loaded with Dove Grey. Pick up Neutral Grey in the dirty brush and paint in the shadows. Highlight the same way with Warm White.

## Berries
The berries are basecoated with a #6 filbert loaded with Cadmium Red. Shade the berries with a 1/4" angle shader sideloaded with Napa Red. Add a bull's eye highlight with a #4 filbert sideloaded Cadmium Red + Warm White 2:1. Brighten with the mix + Warm White 1:1. Smudge in a shine with Warm White. Add dots with Payne's Grey.

The stems are painted with a #2 liner double-loaded with Dove Grey and Neutral Grey. Add Cadmium Red to the dirty brush, and apply tints here and there.

## Finishing
See Painting Terms.

# Roses for the Boudoir

## Palette

**DecoArt Americana**

Bleached Sand
Burnt Sienna Traditional
Celery
Moon Yellow
Plantation Pine
Shale Green
Warm Neutral
Warm White

## Mediums

DecoArt Brush 'N Blend Extender
J.W. Etc. Metallic Finishing Wax: Copper and Gold

## General Information

This study is painted with floats of color directly over the background to form the design elements. There are no individual basecoats.

## Preparation

The tinted bisque is paint-ready. Trace the pattern onto tracing paper and transfer the design onto the pieces. Apply a thin coat of Extender to the tray and box lid. Shade all around the church and flowers with a #14 flat sideloaded with Plantation Pine.

## Church

The shadow areas on the church are painted with an #8 flat sideloaded with Shale Green. Highlight the bright sides of the church with Warm White. Add windows and doors with a #2 flat loaded with a wash of Shale Green + Plantation Pine 1:1. The trim and the cross are painted with a #6/0 liner loaded with thinned Plantation Pine.

## Leaves

The leaves are formed with an #8 flat sideloaded with Celery, along the outside edges and through the middle. Shade the stem end and the center with Celery + Plantation Pine 2:1. Reinforce the shadows with Plantation Pine. Highlight the tips and bright side of the center with Bleached Sand. Veins are painted with a #6/0 liner loaded with Celery + Bleached Sand 1:1.

## Supplies

Tracing paper
Transfer paper
Soft cloth

## Loew-Cornell Brushes

#0, #6/0 liner
#2, #8 #10, #14 flat
#2 filbert

## Surface

Item #168-0022, Nouveau porcelain tray, misty, and item #168-0023, Nouveau porcelain box, misty, available from Viking Woodcrafts, Inc.

## Roses

With a #10 flat sideloaded with Warm Neutral, shade the roses on each petal closest to the center, where the petal comes out from behind another, or where the petal folds over onto itself. Highlight the petals with Bleached Sand. Reinforce the highlight with Warm White.

The centers are washed in with Moon Yellow. Shade the bottoms with an #8 flat sideloaded with Burnt Sienna, and highlight the tops with Bleached Sand. The dots on and around the centers are Burnt Sienna, then Bleached Sand.

Stems and branches are painted with a #0 liner loaded with thinned Burnt Sienna.

Small filler leaves are painted with a #2 filbert double-loaded with Plantation Pine + Celery 1:1.

## Finishing

Embellish the raised edges by dry brushing with Copper metallic wax. Add Gold over the Copper on the highest points. Let set, according to directions, then rub over with a soft cloth.

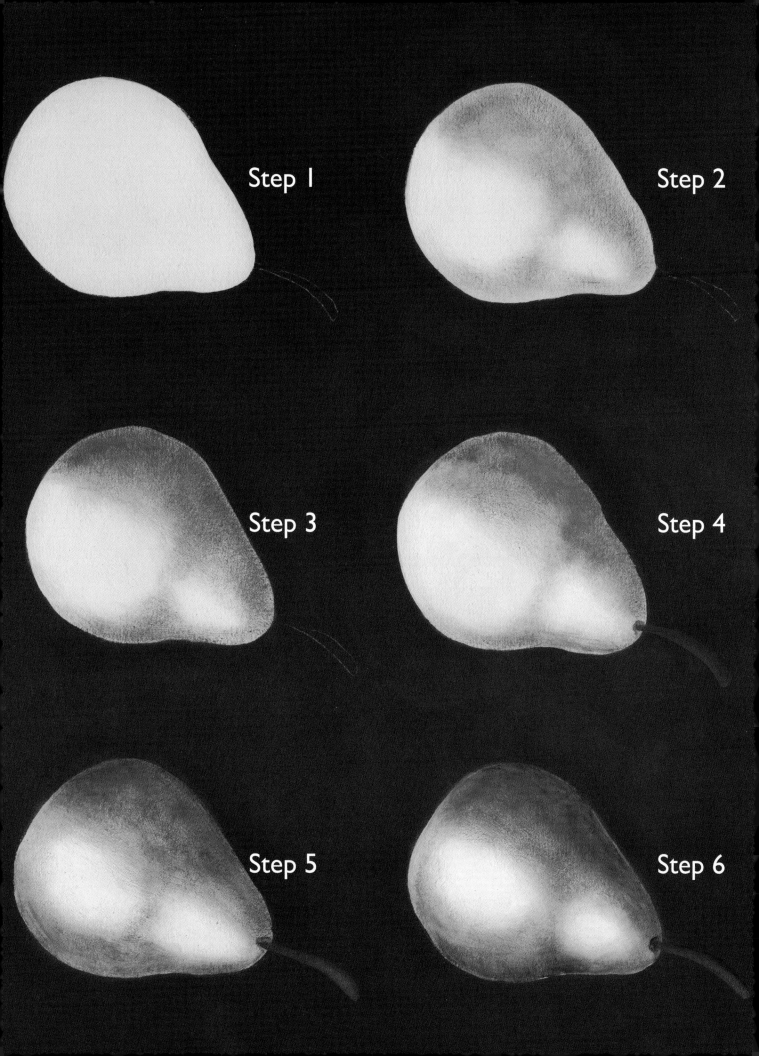

Step 1

Step 2

Step 3

Step 4

Step 5

Step 6

# Sepia Still Life

## Palette

**DecoArt Americana**

Burnt Umber Traditional

Dark Chocolate

French Mocha

Light Mocha

Milk Chocolate

Soft Black

Titanium White

Warm White

**Dazzling Metallics**

Copper

## Mediums

White gesso

DecoArt Brush 'N Blend

Extender

DecoArt Faux

Glazing Medium

## Supplies

Fine-grit sandpaper

Combing tool

Tracing paper

Transfer paper

## Loew-Cornell Brushes

#4 round

#10, #14 flat

#10 filbert

#4, #8 scumbler

1" oval wash

1" and 2" basecoat

## Surface

9" X 16" Harrington canvas and frame, available from The Creative Touch.

## Preparation

Paint the canvas with two coats of white gesso, sanding in between. Paint the canvas with one coat of Dark Chocolate. Let dry. Slip-slap the background, using a 1" oval wash brush, with Faux Glazing Medium, Dark Chocolate, French Mocha, and Light Mocha.

## Frame

Paint the frame with Copper. Add the graining on the frame with Burnt Umber + Faux Glazing Medium 1:1. Tape off one side of the frame and apply the color glaze; while wet, pull a combing tool through the glaze in straight lines from the inside edge. Wipe the combing tool often to remove excess glaze. Let one side dry, tape off the next, and repeat all around the frame. Let dry thoroughly. Tape off a 1/4" border on the outside and inside edge of the frame. Paint these borders, the thin edge on the outside and the inside edge of the frame with Burnt Umber Traditional.

Trace the pattern onto tracing paper. Transfer the outlines onto the canvas. Basecoat the pieces as follows:

## Fruit

Basecoat all the fruit Light Mocha. See Step 1 on the worksheet. Scumble the first shadows with an #8 scumbler sparsely loaded with French Mocha, as in Step 2. Deepen the shadows with French Mocha + Dark Chocolate 2:1. See Step 3. Scumble a highlight with Light Mocha + Warm White 1:1, as in Step 4. Reinforce the highlight with Warm White, as in Step 5.

Leaves and stems are basecoated with Milk Chocolate. Scumble shadows with a #4 scumbler loaded with Dark Chocolate. Scumble the highlight with French Mocha.

## Bowl

The inside of the bowl is painted with Burnt Umber, the outside with Milk Chocolate. Scumble shadows on the outside of the bowl with an #8 scumbler loaded with Dark Chocolate. Reinforce with Burnt Umber. Scumble the highlights with French Mocha. Lightly scumble over the inside and outside of the bowl with Copper.

## Shadows

The second layer of shadows and highlights are painted over an Extender-moistened surface.

Apply a thin coat of Extender over the fruit. Deepen the shadows with a #10 filbert sideloaded with Dark Chocolate. See Step 5. Reinforce with Burnt Umber. Add a bull's eye highlight with Titanium White, as in Step 6. Let dry. Add a reflected light with Titanium White as in Step 6.

The shadows on the leaves are painted with a #10 flat sideloaded with Burnt Umber. Highlight with Copper.

The shadows on the inside and outside of the bowl are painted with a #14 flat sideloaded with Burnt Umber. Deepen the shadows with Soft Black. Add Copper to the highlight area.

The cast shadows around the fruit and bowl are painted over a wet surface; apply a thin coat of Extender and paint the shadows with a #4 round loaded with Soft Black + Extender 1:1.

## Finishing

See Painting Terms.

29

Skating on the Lake

## Palette

### DecoArt Americana

Antique Teal
Black Plum
Brilliant Red
Burnt Sienna
Burnt Umber
Cadmium Yellow
Calypso Blue
Champagne Gold
Cocoa
Fleshtone
French Vanilla
Ice Blue
Lamp Black
Midnite Green
Napa Red
Neutral Grey
Payne's Grey
True Ochre
Uniform Blue
Warm White

## Mediums

DecoArt Faux Glazing Medium
DecoArt Brush 'N Blend Extender
Clear glaze or matte spray sealer
Varnish

## Supplies

Fine-grit sandpaper
Tack cloth
Tracing paper
Transfer paper
24" wreath
3 yards of wired ribbon, 2" wide
A pair of skate laces or 6 yards of 1/8" cording
3 yards #20 gauge florist wire
Hot glue gun
Varnish

## Loew-Cornell Brushes

#1 round
#0, #6/0 liner
#4, #8, #14 flat
3/4" oval wash
1/8" deerfoot

## Surface

Wooden skates, life size, available from The Creative Touch and from Viking Woodcrafts, Inc., item #20-10998.

## Preparation

Sand and seal the skates. Paint the skates Uniform Blue. Paint the runners Champagne Gold.

Slip-slap the skates with a 3/4" oval wash: glaze, Uniform Blue, Payne's Grey, and Ice Blue. Keep the darker tones toward the bottom of the skate. Let dry completely.

Trace the pattern onto tracing paper. Transfer the horizon, snow, and road lines onto the skates. Apply Extender to the skates and pit-pat Payne's Grey into the shadow areas, on both sides of the path, under the house, and all around the edges of the lake. Use Ice Blue in the light areas, on top of snow mounds, and streaks through the middle of the lake. Let dry.

Transfer the houses, people, and foliage.

## General Information

The houses and the characters are painted with a brush that has been moistened with Extender before loading with paint. The shadows and highlights are painted while the basecoat is still wet, with each color sideloaded onto the dirty brush.

## Houses

Paint the tan house with an #8 flat loaded with Cocoa + Neutral Grey, brush-mixed. Shade with Burnt Umber. The door is Burnt Sienna; shade with Burnt Umber. The roof is Lamp Black; highlight with Ice Blue. The trim is painted with a #6/0 liner loaded with thinned Warm White + a touch of Cocoa.

The red house is painted with Napa Red and shaded with Lamp Black. The doors are Cocoa, shaded with Burnt Umber. The roof is Neutral Grey, shaded with Lamp Black and highlighted with Ice Blue. The trim is Ice Blue.

The green house is painted with Antique Teal + a touch of Payne's Grey and shaded with Payne's Grey. The roof is Neutral Grey, shaded with Lamp Black and highlighted with Ice Blue. The trim is Ice Blue.

## All houses

The dark windows are painted with a small flat loaded with Lamp Black. The lighted windows are painted with the brush double-loaded with True Ochre and Brilliant Red. The chimneys

are Burnt Sienna, shaded with Burnt Umber. The smoke from the chimneys is painted with a #4 flat sideloaded with Ice Blue.

## Bushes and Trees

The bushes are stippled with a 1/8" deerfoot double-loaded with Midnite Green and Antique Teal; pick up Ice Blue on the light side, and tap in a highlight.

The bare trees are painted with a #0 liner double-loaded with Burnt Umber and Burnt Sienna; stroke in a few highlights with Ice Blue.

## Streetlights

Streetlights are painted Lamp Black; over-stroke here and there with Ice Blue. The flame is painted with a #1 round double-loaded with Brilliant Red and True Ochre.

## Sleigh

The sleigh is painted with Napa Red, shaded with Black Plum, and highlighted with Brilliant Red. The runners are Lamp Black. The horse is painted with Burnt Umber and highlighted with Burnt Sienna. Stroke in the mane with Burnt Sienna, the tail with Burnt Sienna and Burnt Umber. The livery is Lamp Black; the rod is Cocoa.

## People

All of the people are painted with a #1 round brush moistened with Extender. The colors follow for all clothing and faces. Refer to the photo for colors used.

## Skin

Fleshtone, shaded with Burnt Sienna, highlighted with Warm White.

## Hair

Hair is stroked in with the darker color and over-stroked with the lighter color. Brown tones are Burnt Umber and Burnt Sienna; blonde tones are Burnt Sienna and True Ochre.

## Clothing

Tan is Cocoa + Neutral Grey 2:1, shaded with Burnt Umber and highlighted with French Vanilla.

Brown is Burnt Umber shaded with Lamp Black, highlighted with Cocoa.

Red is Napa Red, shaded with Black Plum and highlighted with Brilliant Red.

Green is Antique Teal, shaded with Payne's Grey and highlighted Ice Blue.

Grey is Neutral Grey, shaded with Lamp Black and highlighted with Warm White.

Black is Lamp Black, highlighted with Calypso Blue.

White is Warm White, shaded with Ice Blue.

Skates are Lamp Black, highlighted with Calypso Blue.

## Bench and Fence

The bench and the fence are Burnt Umber, highlighted with Burnt Sienna. The metal arms and legs on the bench are Lamp Black.

## Lanterns

Hand-held lanterns are painted the same as the streetlights (black with over-strokes here and there of Ice Blue), with the addition of a candle that is painted Warm White.

## Finishing

Apply a thin coat of Extender to the skates. Add more highlights to the snow with a #14 flat sideloaded with Warm White. Make some scuff marks under the skaters with Ice Blue. Add a glow around the lamps with Cadmium Yellow. Let dry thoroughly, then varnish.

## Assembly

Cut a length of 2" wide ribbon to fit around the center of the wreath, and glue in place. Make a bow with the remaining ribbon and attach to the wreath with wire. Lace the skates with the laces or cording and wire them to the wreath with the florist wire. Add additional decorations as desired.

# Spring Welcome Banner

## Palette
**DecoArt Americana**
Black Green
Cadmium Yellow
Canyon Orange
Cool White
Deep Midnight Blue
Forest Green
Mistletoe
Pumpkin
Soft Lilac
Taffy Cream
Violet Haze

## Mediums
DecoArt Brush 'N Blend Extender
DecoArt Faux Glazing Medium

## Supplies
Tracing paper
Transfer paper
3" to 4" paint roller
White craft glue
Scissors
Soft cloth
Exterior varnish

## Loew-Cornell Brushes
#4 round
#20, 1" flat
1/2", 3/4", 1 1/2" oval wash
1/4" deerfoot

## Surface
Item #140-2013, Spring Banner Kit, which includes: 17" X 30" floor cloth canvas, 2 2" wooden ball finials, 19" X 1/2" dowel rod, 1/8" piece of cork, and 24" cording, available from The Creative Touch and Viking Woodcrafts, Inc., item #20-10999.

## Preparation
The canvas is primed and ready to paint. Paint the entire canvas with the roller, loaded with Black Green. Let dry.

## Background
Slip-slap the canvas with a 1 1/2" oval wash with a mixture of Faux Glazing Medium + Extender 6:1, Black Green, Forest Green, and Mistletoe.

Trace the patterns onto tracing paper. Transfer the flowers onto the bottom of the canvas. The lettering should be 4" from the top edge. Don't trim the excess around the flowers at this time. Transfer the shapes of the bees onto the cork. Cut the shapes out with a pair of scissors.

## Crocus
Tip: The use of two colors for basecoating immediately establishes shadows and highlights. Use some Extender in the brush to help the flow of paint and the blending of colors to eliminate lines or ridges. The use of filberts for petals provides soft edges and smoother transition of color.

Basecoat the flower petals with a 3/4" oval wash for large petals and 1/2" oval wash for smaller petals, moistened with Extender and loaded with Violet Haze in the dark areas and Soft Lilac in the light areas. Let dry.

Apply a thin coat of Extender over the petals. Add shadows with a 1" flat that has been moistened in Extender and sideloaded with Violet Haze + Deep Midnight Blue 1:1. Use a #20 flat for smaller petals. Add highlights with a 3/4" oval wash sideloaded with Cool White + a touch of Soft Lilac.

## Stamens
Pull the stem of the stamen with a #4 round loaded with Canyon Orange. Tap in Canyon Orange, Pumpkin, and then Taffy Cream over the tops of the stamens with a 1/4" deerfoot.

## Leaves
Leaves are painted with a #4 round double-loaded with Forest Green and Black Green. Pick up some Mistletoe on one side of the dirty brush and add a highlight stroke.

### Lettering

Paint the letters with Pumpkin. Shade in all the folds with Canyon Orange. Highlight with Pumpkin + Taffy Cream 1:1. Add stylus dots on the sides of each letter with Pumpkin.

### Cork Cutouts

The bees are painted with mixes of paint and faux glaze 1:1. The head and dark stripes are Black Green. The light stripes are Taffy Cream, and the wings are Cool White + a touch of Pumpkin. Shade the dark stripes with Black Green, the light stripes and the wings with Pumpkin + Taffy Cream 2:1.

### Dowel and Finials

Stain the dowel and the finials with Violet Haze + Faux Glazing Medium 1:1. Antique the finials with Deep Midnight Blue + Extender 1:1. Wipe away the excess with a soft cloth.

### Finishing

Carefully cut the banner along the bottom in the shapes of the flowers.

Apply a heavy layer of glue to the back of each cork cutout. Place on the banner and press firmly. Wipe away excess glue from around the cutout, and place a weight on top until it dries.

Apply a generous amount of glue to the top edge of the banner. Fold over approximately 2" from the top, press firmly, and place a weight on top, as with the cutouts.

Apply multiple coats of exterior varnish to the front and back sides of the banner and on the finials.

Note: The application of varnish to the back side prevents the banner from curling.

### Assembly

Push the dowel through the rod pocket at the top of the banner; apply glue to the ends, and press into the holes drilled in the finial. Attach the cord to the dowel rod.

Winter Welcome Banner

## *Palette*
### DecoArt Americana
Black Plum
Brilliant Red
Burnt Sienna
Hauser Dark Green
Hauser Light Green
Ice Blue
Leaf Green
Mistletoe
Napa Red
True Ochre
Warm White

Hot Shots Fiery Red
Hot Shots Scorching Yellow

## *Mediums*
DecoArt Brush 'N Blend Extender
DecoArt Faux Glazing Medium

## *Supplies*
Tracing paper
Transfer paper
3" to 4" paint roller
White craft glue
Scissors
Soft cloth
Exterior varnish

## *Loew-Cornell Brushes*
#3 round
#8, #10, #12, 14, #20 flat
1 1/2" oval wash
#2 duster

## *Surface*
#140-2014 Winter banner kit, which in-
cludes: 17" X 30" floor cloth canvas, 2
2" wooden ball finials, 19" X 1/2"
dowel rod, 1/8" cork, round plugs,
and 24" cording, available from
The Creative Touch and Viking
Woodcrafts, Inc., item
#20-11000.